Rookie
Read-About® Holidays

100th Day
of School

By Melissa Schiller

Consultant
Don L. Curry
Reading and Content Consultant

Children's Press®
A Division of Scholastic Inc.
New York   Toronto   London   Auckland   Sydney
Mexico City   New Delhi   Hong Kong
Danbury, Connecticut

Designer: Herman Adler Design
Photo Researcher: Caroline Anderson
The photo on the cover shows three children in 100th Day hats.

Library of Congress Cataloging–in–Publication Data

Schiller, Melissa.
  100th day of school / by Melissa Schiller ; consultant, Don Curry.
      p. cm. – (Rookie read-about holidays)
Includes index.
Summary: Describes ways of celebrating the one hundredth day of school,
such as making hats with one hundred stickers, being quiet for one
hundred seconds, and recycling one hundred cans.
  ISBN 0-516-25856-7 (lib. bdg.)   0-516-27943-2 (pbk.)
 1. Hundred (The number)–Juvenile literature. 2. Special
days–Juvenile literature. [1. Hundred (The number) 2. Special days.]
I. Title: One hundredth day of school. II. Title. III. Series.
  QA141.15.S32 2003
  513.2'11–dc21
                              2003000463

Today is the 100th day of school!

3

We have been counting since the first day of school. Today we will celebrate (SEL-uh-brate).

5

We make hats for the special day. We use paper, scissors, and stickers. Each hat has 100 stickers on it.

We put our handprints on a banner. There are 100 handprints. Can you count them?

We put 100 pieces of
cereal on a string to make
a necklace (NEK-liss).

We made a paper chain
to hang around the room.
There are 10 colors. Can
you name them?

12

We tell 100 jokes.
We laugh a lot.

We count 100 cubes (kyoobs). Then we use a ruler to see how long they are.

15

We did not talk for 100 seconds! We looked at the clock. It was hard to be so quiet.

We recycle (ree-SYE-kuhl) 100 cans.

19

How many jumping jacks
can you do in 100 seconds?
Can you hop on one foot
100 times?

Touch your toes 100 times!

Here is a puzzle with 100 pieces. We work to put it all together.

24

We make 100 paper airplanes. We test which ones can fly the farthest.

When we count to 100,
we make groups of 10.
In each bag there are:

 10 beads

 10 snacks

 10 balls

 10 feathers

10 stickers

 10 buttons

 10 noodles

 10 crayons

 10 cars

 10 dolls

Now it is time for a parade. We put on our hats. We shout and smile as we celebrate our 100th day.

How do you celebrate the
100th day of school?

Words You Know

cereal

cubes

handprints

paper hats

parade

puzzle

recycle

Index

About the Author

Melissa Schiller taught elementary school for five years and has written a number of children's books. She lives in New York City and has two sons, ages two and four, who are her inspiration for writing.

Photo Credits

Photographs © 2003: Corbis Images: 24 (Stephen S.T. Bradley), 11 (Jose Luis Pelaez, Inc.); Dubuque Community Schools/Gary Olsen: cover, 6; Ellen B. Senisi: 15, 30 top right; PhotoDisc/Getty Images/Andersen Ross: 16; PhotoEdit/David Young-Wolff: 10, 30 top left; Stock Boston: 9, 30 bottom left (Bob Daemmrich), 12 (Gregg Mancuso), 28, 31 top (Lawrence Migdale); The Image Bank/Getty Images/David Zelick: 29; The Image Works: 23, 31 bottom left (Elizabeth Crews), 19, 20, 21, 31 bottom right (Bob Daemmrich).

Illustrations by Paul Rowntree

WALLY

THE LIFE OF A
PUNNY BUNNY

MOLLY PROTTAS

CLARKSON POTTER/PUBLISHERS
NEW YORK

All rights reserved.
Published in the United States by Clarkson Potter/
Publishers, an imprint of the Crown Publishing Group,
a division of Penguin Random House LLC, New York.
crownpublishing.com
clarksonpotter.com

CLARKSON POTTER is a trademark and POTTER with
colophon is a registered trademark of Penguin Random
House LLC.

Library of Congress Cataloging-in-Publication Data
is available upon request.

ISBN 978-0-451-49590-7
Ebook ISBN 978-0-451-49591-4

Printed in China

Book and cover design by Danielle Deschenes
Book and cover photographs by Jack Deutsch
Book and cover illustrations by woolypear

10 9 8 7 6 5 4 3 2 1

First Edition

INTRODUCTION

Hi! It's ME, Wally! What I'm about to declare may astound you. Are you ready? . . . I'm a BUNNY! I've been mistaken for a puppy, a poodle, a lamb, a moose, and even a pom-pom and a stuffed animal.

While I'm delighted by these creative interpretations, I've developed an enormous sense of pride in my bunnyhood. If you've visited me on Instagram, you know I'm silly and imaginative and that I love to laugh. And nothing tickles me more than bunny puns!

I've challenged myself to keep a straight face while reading this book, and I can't make it past even the second page without erupting in giggles! Can you? I'm **HOP**ful that you'll go **PUN**anas for this book!

THIS IS WALLY THE BUNNY.

WALLY THE BUNNY

LIKES TO COOK.

—◄≡★≡►—

WHEN HE MAKES AN
OMELET, HE STARTS BY
WHISKERING AN EGG.

WALLY THE BUNNY

LIKES THE CITY.

——◄✷★✷►——

HE'S USED TO
HERBAN LIVING.

WALLY THE BUNNY

LIKES TO DRIVE.

SOMETIMES HE ACTS

AS A CHAU**FUR**.

WALLY THE BUNNY

LIKES MUSIC.

HIS FAVORITE KIND IS
HIP-**HOP**.

WALLY THE BUNNY

LIKES TO COLLECT RECORDS.

———✦★✦———

HE LISTENS TO ALBUMS
ON HIS **TURNIP** TABLES.

WALLY THE BUNNY

LIKES TO PERFORM.

WHEN HE'S OUT ON THE TOWN
HE SINGS **CARROT**OKE.

WALLY THE BUNNY
ALSO LIKES
INSTRUMENTS.

HE'S LEARNING TO PLAY
THE **HOP**SICHORD.

WALLY THE BUNNY
LIKES TO PLAY THE DRUMS.

HE REALLY **DIGS**
THE **BEETS**.

WALLY THE BUNNY
LIKES TO DANCE.

HIS FAVORITE MOVE IS
THE **CABBAGE PATCH**.

WALLY THE BUNNY
LIKES TO SEE SHOWS.

HE ENJOYS THEM EVEN
WHEN THEY FLOP.

WALLY THE BUNNY

LIKES TO WRITE.

————⊰✦⊱————

WHEN HE GROWS UP,
HE WANTS TO BE A
GNAWVELIST.

WALLY THE BUNNY
LIKES TO READ.

HE OFTEN **BURROWS**
BOOKS FROM THE
LIBRARY.

WALLY THE BUNNY

LIKES STORIES.

HIS FAVORITE KIND ARE

COTTON TAILS.

WALLY THE BUNNY

LIKES TO BE CREATIVE.

HE OFTEN THINKS
OUTSIDE THE BOX.

WALLY THE BUNNY

LIKES TO PAINT.

━━ ✳ ★ ✳ ━━

HE'S A
TAILENTED ARTIST.

WALLY THE BUNNY

LIKES HEALTHY FOOD.

——✦ ★ ✦——

HE'S ESPECIALLY
GRAPEFUL FOR FRUIT.

WALLY THE BUNNY
LIKES SANDWICHES.

HIS FAVORITES ARE
ALWAYS MADE
WITH TWO **BUNS**
(AT LEAST).

WALLY THE BUNNY

LIKES TO EXPLORE.

HE HAS PERFORMED MANY
FEETS OF DARING.

WALLY THE BUNNY

LIKES TO PLAY SOCCER.

HIS FAVORITE
POSITION IS DE**FENCE**.

WALLY THE BUNNY
LIKES TO LOOK COOL.

WHEN HE GOES TO THE
STYLIST, HE GETS A
HAREDO.

WALLY THE BUNNY

LIKES TO BE CLEAN.

IF HE'S DIRTY,
HE'LL **PAWS** TO WASH
HIMSELF.

WALLY THE BUNNY
LIKES TO USE A COMPASS.

—◦✶◦—

DEPENDING WHAT IT SAYS,
HE'LL GO WEST
OR HE'LL GO **EAST**ER.

WALLY THE BUNNY LIKES TO TRAVEL.

CHEW-CHEW TRAINS
ARE HIS FAVORITE.

pet the bunny

WALLY THE BUNNY

LIKES TO BE PET.

HE'S **WOOLY,**
WOOLY SOFT.

WALLY THE BUNNY

LIKES PUBLIC SPEAKING.

HE KNOWS WHEN TO
OPEN HIS MOUTH.

WALLY THE BUNNY

LIKES TO LEARN.

HE **NOSE** A LOT.

WALLY THE BUNNY

LIKES SCHOOL.

SOMETIMES HIS
HOMEWORK CAN BE
TUFT.

WALLY THE BUNNY

LIKES TO BE HONEST.

HE ALWAYS

TELLS THE **TOOTH**.

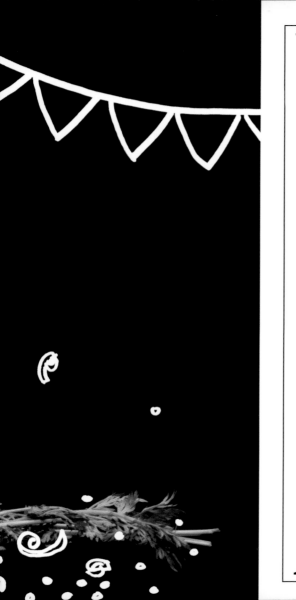

WALLY THE BUNNY

LIKES TO BE HAPPY.

HE BELIEVES JOY
IS AT THE **ROOT** OF
EVERYTHING.

WALLY THE BUNNY

LIKES TO GO TO PARTIES.

HIS FAVORITE FESTIVE DRINK
IS A **BUNNY** MARY.

WALLY THE BUNNY

LIKES POP CULTURE.

━━➤✦★✦◄━━

WHEN HE'S MISTAKEN
FOR OTHER CELEBRITIES,
IT REALLY **BUGS** HIM.

WALLY THE BUNNY
LIKES TO LISTEN TO
HIS FRIENDS.

———✦ ★ ✦———

WHEN THEY TALK,
HE'S **ALL EARS**.

WALLY THE BUNNY

LIKES TO BE POLITE.

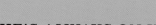

HE'S ALWAYS ON HIS
BEST BE**HAY**VIOR.

WALLY THE BUNNY

LIKES YOU.

HE'S A **BERRY** NICE BUNNY.

ACKNOWLEDGMENTS

Thank you to the wonderful team of people who contributed to this book, including my agent, Alison Fargis, of Stonesong Literary Agency; photographer Jack Deutsch; and the team at Clarkson Potter: my editor, Amanda Englander, designer Danielle Deschenes, and Emma Brodie, Kevin Garcia, Patricia Shaw, Natasha Martin, and Kevin Sweeting. Writing this book has been an incredible opportunity and an inspiring journey.

Thank you especially to my delightful, encouraging, compassionate, and loyal followers. "Wally's *here* for you" because you have been here for him.

To all the famous cats and dogs who have been willing to share the limelight with a bunny, thank you.

Thank you to everyone who has ever listened to me, or pretended to listen to me, as I talked about my bunnies and celebrated their glory.

Last, thank you to my family for supporting me, laughing with me, and being my water wings when the seas got rough. And in particular, thank you to my sister and chief advisor, Rachel (aka Wachy).

ABOUT THE AUTHOR

Like Wally, Molly Prottas has a creative spirit and loves to write about her real and imaginary adventures with Wally on their Instagram page. You can find them at @wally_and_molly. She is equally passionate about her career as a clinical social worker with a focus in children's mental health. If you are considering a pet rabbit, please visit rabbit.org to learn more about the responsibilities involved in caring for these special animals.

the end